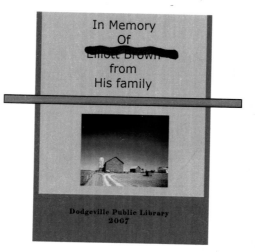

In Memory
Of
Elliott Brown
from
His family

Dodgeville Public Library
2007

GETTING INTO NATURE™

GETTING INTO NATURE™

Corn

INSIDE AND OUT

Text by Andrew Hipp
Illustrations by Andrea Ricciardi di Gaudesi

The Rosen Publishing Group's
PowerKids Press™
New York

To Dr. Hugh Iltis, for inspiration, encouragement, and generosity

Published in 2004 in North America
by The Rosen Publishing Group, Inc.
29 East 21st Street, New York, NY 10010

Book Design:
Andrea Dué s.r.l., Florence, Italy

Illustrations:
Andrea Ricciardi di Gaudesi and Studio Stalio
Map by Alessandro Bartolozzi

Scientific Advice for Botanical Illustrations:
Riccardo Maria Baldini

Library of Congress Cataloging-in-Publication Data
Hipp, Andrew.
Corn inside and out / Andrew Hipp.
    p. cm. — (Getting into nature)
Summary: Relates the history of corn and its various uses and
examines the plant's appearance, structure, growth, and development.
Includes bibliographical references and index.
ISBN 0-8239-4205-8 (lib. bdg.)
1. Corn—Juvenile literature. [1. Corn.] I. Title. II. Series.
SB191.M2H63 2004
633.1'5—dc22
                                                    2003015536

Manufactured in Italy by Eurolitho S.p.A., Milan

Contents

Maize: Corn of the Native Americans

Most of the world's food comes from seven kinds of grasses—wheat, rice, rye, oats, barley, sorghum, and corn. Corn is the most widely planted **cereal** crop in the world next to wheat. It grows on every continent except for Antarctica. Christopher Columbus, the European explorer who "discovered" America, found corn on his first trip to the New World in 1492. Two of his sailors visited the island of Cuba and brought back several ears of corn. Columbus brought these ears back to Europe. Portuguese sailors then carried corn to China in 1516. Soon the plant spread by trade to Africa, India, Turkey, and the rest of the world.

Today, corn is the most important food crop in many parts of the world, including Mexico, and an important part of American farming and business. The word "corn" comes from an Old English word that meant "grain." Today, the word "corn" refers to grainy cereals in Germany and wheat in England.

Corn or maize
(Zea mays)

The corn plant is one of the world's largest grasses. Fully grown plants are often taller than a human being—up to 20 feet (6 meters) tall in Central America—with an ear that may be 1 foot (0.3 m) or longer.

Corn, From Root to Tassel

The stem of a corn plant is built of long pipelike **internodes** filled with spongy **pith** and slender tubes that carry water and food. Between the internodes are woody rings called **nodes**. Roots curve downward from the lowest nodes, holding the tall corn plant up against the weight of the ears and the wind. Leaves grow from the upper nodes. The bottom half of each leaf wraps around the stem, forming a **sheath**, or tight covering. The leaf blade spreads away from the plant to capture sunlight. Snug within the leaf sheaths near the middle of the stem are one or more ears of corn. The ears are held up on a short, thick stem, called the **shank**, and wrapped inside special leaf sheaths that make up the husk. At the very top of the plant is a branched collection of male, or boy, flowers, called the **tassel**.

ears

stem, surrounded by a leaf sheath

roots

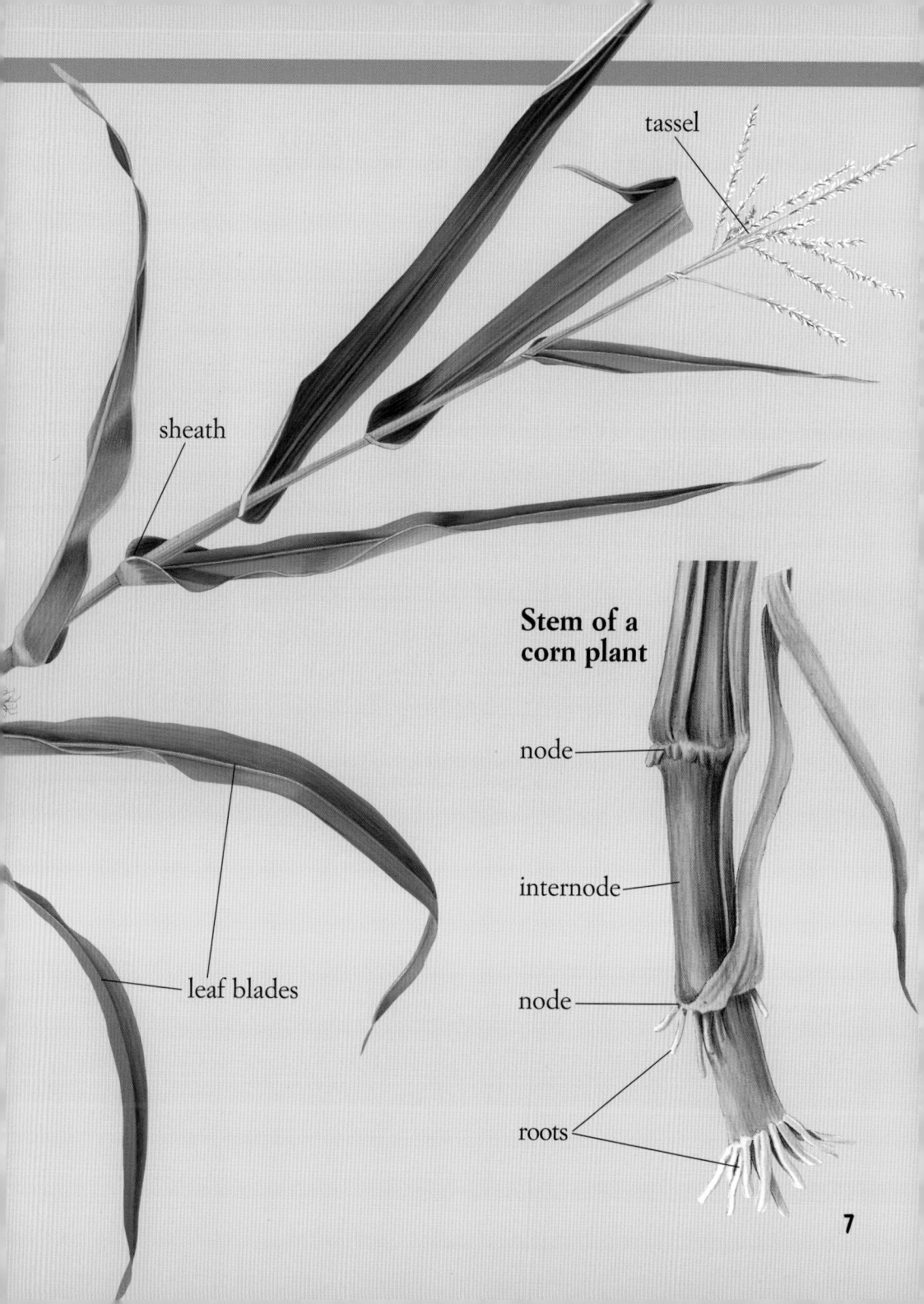

tassel

sheath

Stem of a corn plant

node

internode

node

roots

leaf blades

How Corn Plants Grow

Long, narrow tubes inside most evergreens, grasses, and other flowering plants carry water and **minerals** from the soil up to the rest of the plant. These tubes, called **vessels**, connect with each other end-to-end from the roots to the tips of each leaf, like long straws. While vessels draw water and minerals up, tiny holes in the plant's leaves and stem allow the plant to get fresh air. These holes act like our nostrils, or nose openings. **Chlorophyll**, which gives plants their green color, uses sunlight to turn water and air into sugar. This sugar feeds the entire plant and fills the kernels, or grains, of corn with food.

In corn, much of the sugar produced is first stored in the pith of the stem. When corn ears are close to harvest in August and September, sugar moves quickly from the stem to the ears, where it fills up the kernels.

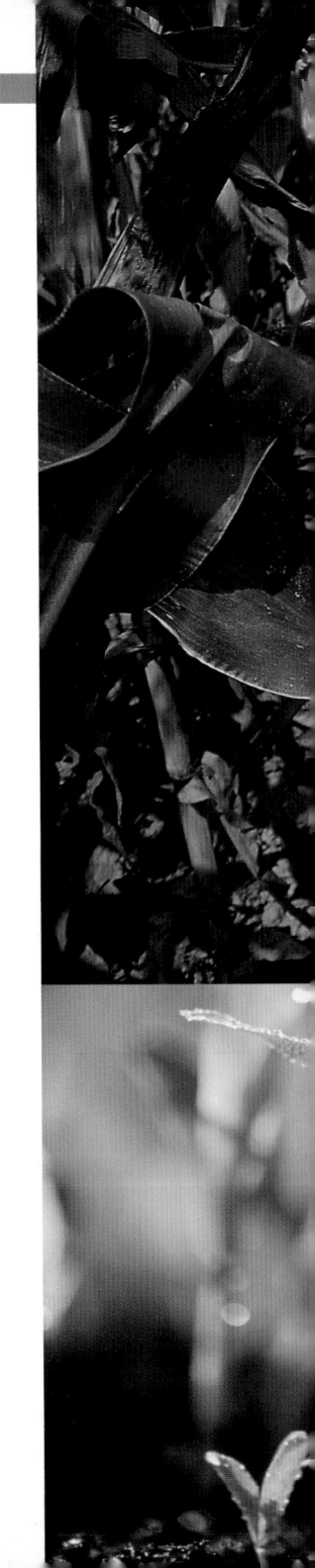

Above: Sugars stored in the stems of full-grown plants are sent to the kernels of the ear, providing food to the baby corn plants inside the kernels and giving kernels their sweet taste.

Left: Two corn seedlings come up out of the soil and put out their first leaves. The air and sunlight these leaves collect will help the seedlings grow into tall plants.

Female Flowers on Ears of Corn

Corn flowers grow in pairs. An ear of corn is made of 4 to 20 or more paired rows of female, or girl, flowers. They are joined to a tough cob. The ear is joined to the stem by a strong branch called a shank. The ear and shank are wrapped inside a tight wrapping of green leaf sheaths, called husks. Husks grow from nodes of the shank, like the plant's leaves grow from nodes of the main stem. Each female flower grows into a kernel of corn that contains an **embryo** and endosperm. The parent plant fills the endosperm with sugar to feed the embryo, which absorbs the food through its scutellum. Coming out of the top of the husks are soft, thin, hairlike threads called **silks**. Each silk connects to a single female flower or kernel. There are as many silks in an ear as there are flowers or kernels.

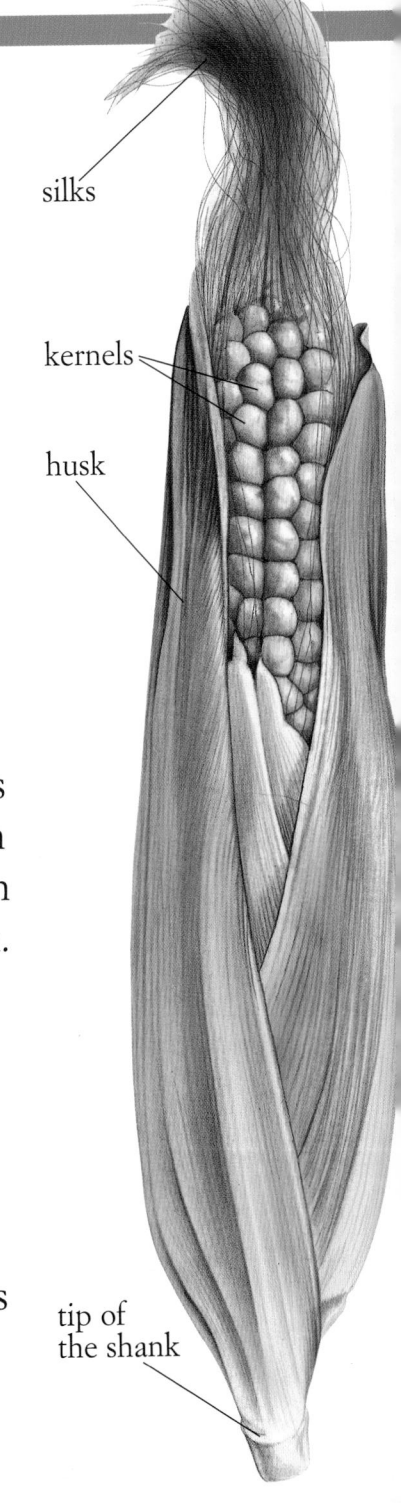

silks

kernels

husk

tip of the shank

10

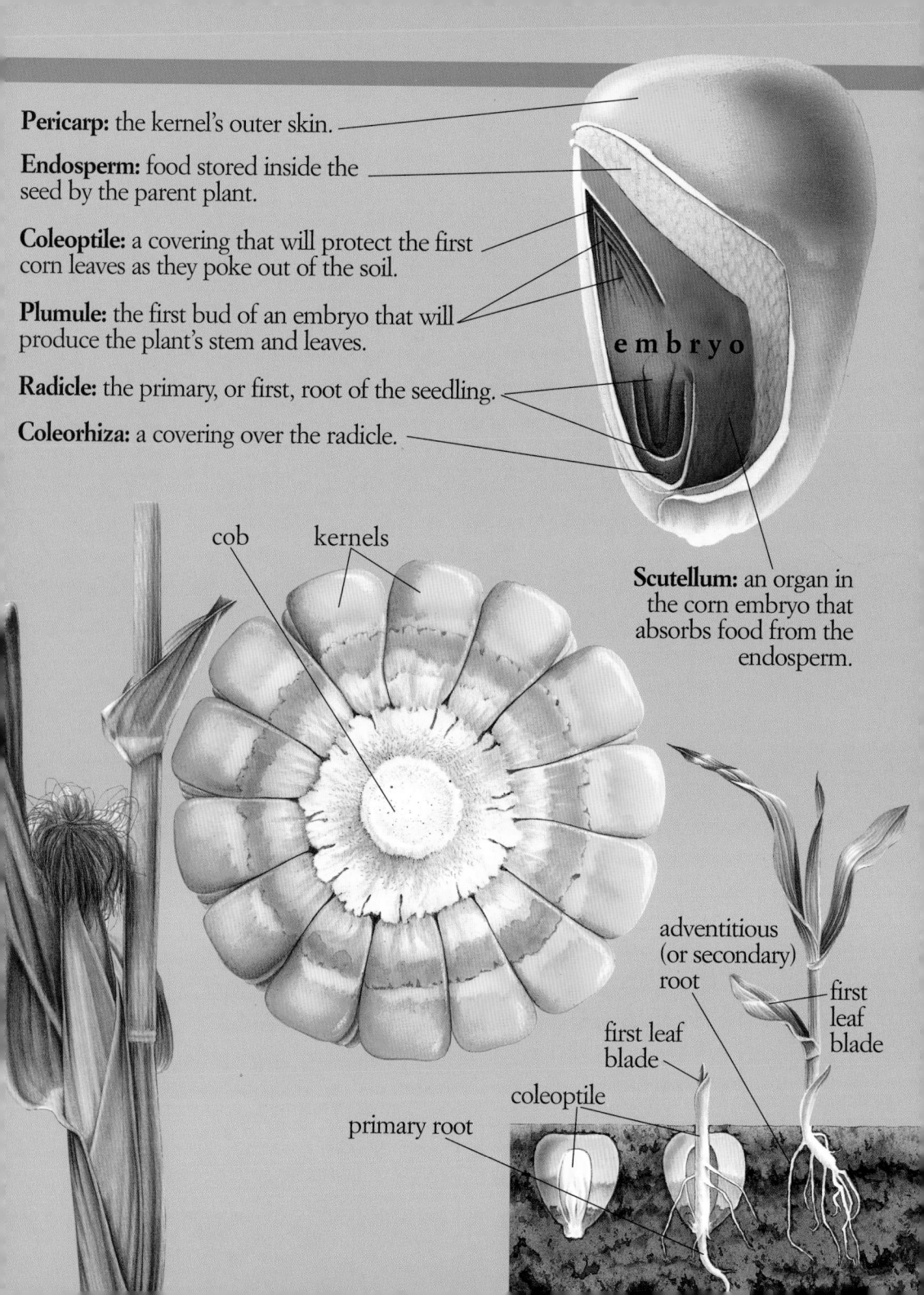

Pericarp: the kernel's outer skin.

Endosperm: food stored inside the seed by the parent plant.

Coleoptile: a covering that will protect the first corn leaves as they poke out of the soil.

Plumule: the first bud of an embryo that will produce the plant's stem and leaves.

Radicle: the primary, or first, root of the seedling.

Coleorhiza: a covering over the radicle.

e m b r y o

Scutellum: an organ in the corn embryo that absorbs food from the endosperm.

cob

kernels

adventitious (or secondary) root

first leaf blade

first leaf blade

coleoptile

primary root

Male Flowers on the Tassel

The tassel atop a corn plant is made of hundreds of male flowers that grow in pairs. Each male flower has three **anthers**, which hang on thin threads. Each anther makes many hundreds of **pollen grains**. Pollen is a dustlike material that helps create new plants. When the pollen grains are ripe, the anthers split open. Wind then carries clouds of pollen from the anthers. Most pollen lands on the ground or on leaves of nearby plants, but some pollen gets caught in tiny hairs on the silks of female flowers. Pollen grains that land on a silk grow a long, narrow tube that digs into the silk. The pollen tube tunnels through the silk, which may be 5 to 15 inches (13 to 38 centimeters) long, into the center of the female flower, where it reaches a single **ovule**, or egg. Here, a seed from the pollen grain combines with an ovule to produce an embryo. This process is called **fertilization**. Each female flower is fertilized by one pollen grain to form a single kernel of corn.

Left: Corn flowers grow paired in structures called spikelets, and the spikelets themselves grow in pairs. This illustration shows a single spikelet. The anthers in one of the flowers in this illustration are ripe and hang down on thread-like filaments.

tassel

The corn tassel is similar in several ways to the corn ear. Male corn flowers grow in pairs, and so do female corn flowers. Male corn spikelets grow in pairs, and so do female corn spikelets. Corn varieties with many rows of kernels on each ear form tassels with pairs of spikelets that grow very close together.

stem

leaf blade

13

Insects Feed on Corn

Corn feeds people and the animals we raise. It also feeds insects, which can cause problems for farmers.

The Southwestern corn borer is the caterpillar of a small, white, Mexican moth that had spread across much of the Great Plains by the 1940s. Corn borers chew holes in leaves, stems, and shanks. The holes they leave can weaken the plant, causing it to bend over. Their chewing also breaks vessels and tubes, so the plant cannot get as much sugar and water as it needs to grow.

The corn rootworm is the **larva** of a beetle that lays hundreds of eggs at a time in the soil of cornfields. The eggs lie in the soil over winter and hatch, or break open, in the spring. The larvae that appear feed on the roots of the corn plants. These plants often either die or produce small ears.

The caterpillars of monarch butterflies feed on milkweed plants, which often grow along the edges of corn fields. A monarch butterfly is seen above.

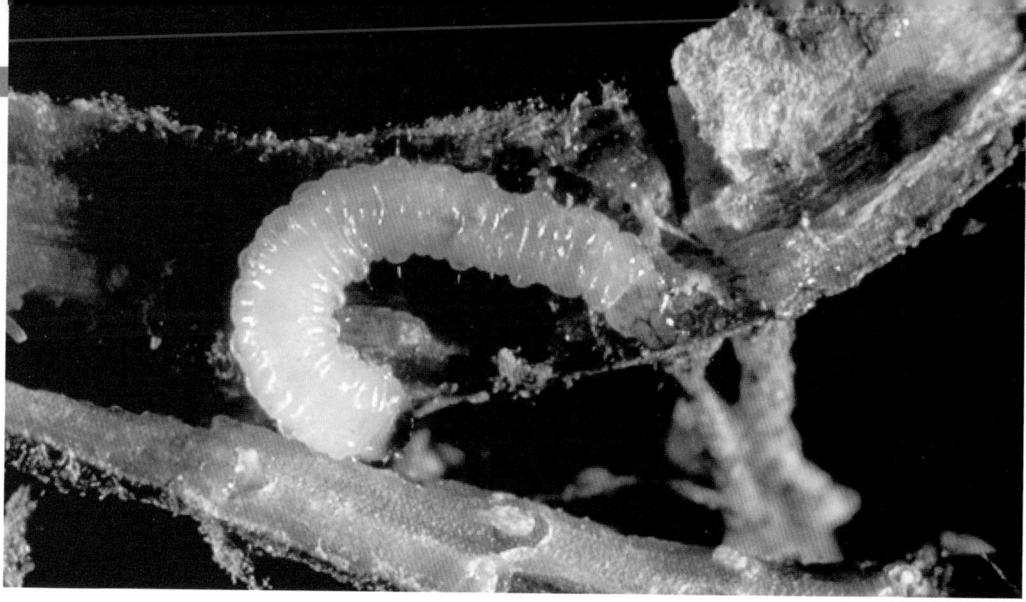

While many caterpillars do corn plants no harm, some modern corn plants developed by scientists may do harm to caterpillars. Recently developed corn plants that produce poisons to kill rootworm caterpillars (*above*) and Southwestern corn borer caterpillars (*below*) also produce poisonous pollen.

This pollen can land on nearby milkweed plants, which are the only food of monarch butterfly caterpillars.

Some scientists have shown that this pollen can harm the monarch butterfly caterpillars as they are feeding on the milkweed.

Modern Corn Comes from Teosinte

Around 8,000 years ago, native Mexicans began to grow a tall grass called teosinte, the ancestor of corn. Teosinte has wide leaves and a big tassel, just like corn. But where corn ears are large with many paired rows of kernels, the ears of teosinte have two single rows of five to twelve kernels. Each kernel is wrapped within a very hard covering called a fruitcase, which is not easily broken open, making the grain almost useless as food.

People may have first grown teosinte for the tasty sugars that the young plant stores in the pith within its stem. You can taste stored sugar in the stem of a young corn plant, which tastes much like sugarcane. After many years, someone found a **mutant** without the tough fruitcases. Only then could people grow teosinte as a cereal crop with grains that could be eaten. Over many

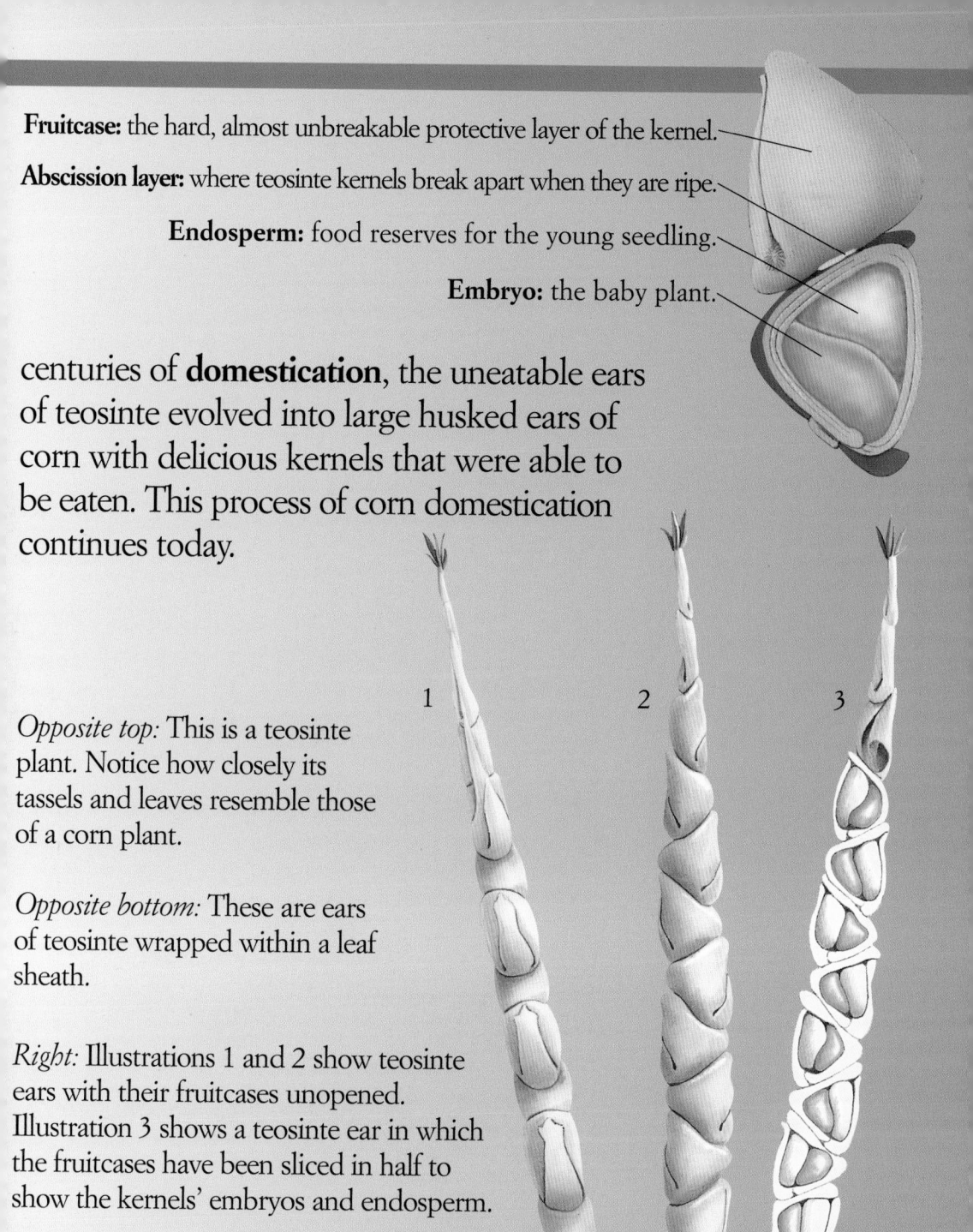

Fruitcase: the hard, almost unbreakable protective layer of the kernel.

Abscission layer: where teosinte kernels break apart when they are ripe.

Endosperm: food reserves for the young seedling.

Embryo: the baby plant.

centuries of **domestication**, the uneatable ears of teosinte evolved into large husked ears of corn with delicious kernels that were able to be eaten. This process of corn domestication continues today.

Opposite top: This is a teosinte plant. Notice how closely its tassels and leaves resemble those of a corn plant.

Opposite bottom: These are ears of teosinte wrapped within a leaf sheath.

Right: Illustrations 1 and 2 show teosinte ears with their fruitcases unopened. Illustration 3 shows a teosinte ear in which the fruitcases have been sliced in half to show the kernels' embryos and endosperm.

1   2   3

The Spread of Mexican Corn

1   2   3   4   5   6

13   14

Corn spread from Mexico to the mountains of South America, where it allowed a rich society to grow. People built corn gardens on the sides of the mountains and ditches to bring water to the growing plants. Each fall, they would till the fields using a flat wooden stick, called the *taclla*. Before planting, the leader would scatter ground corn

on the field and dig the first hole with a golden plow, a tool that digs up soil. In May of the following year, the people would gather the corn. They would bring a part of it to the temple. Another part they would store in giant pots made of clay and straw. Some of the stored corn would be eaten, while some would be saved as seed to be planted the next year.

SOME MEXICAN CORN

1. Tabloncillo blanco
2. Cacahuacintle
3. Chatino maizón
4. Reventador
5. Serrano jalisciense
6. Conejo
7. Mixteco
8. Bolita
9. Nal Tel
10. Oloton
11. Zapalote chico
12. Maíz ancho
13. Zapalote grande
14. Elotes occidentales

Growing and Storing Corn

For thousands of years, the ancient Mexicans and then the North American Indians planted corn in mounds, often with beans and squash. The bean plants would grow up the corn stem, providing beans for people to eat and adding to the soil an element called nitrogen. The nitrogen kept the soil healthy, helping all the plants that were growing there. The squash vines would grow on the ground between the corn plants, shading out weeds.

Months later the corn was ready to be harvested, or gathered. Some corn was harvested while the kernels were white and fleshy inside and good for eating. The rest was harvested later, after the kernels ripened. Much of this corn was stored in baskets either in people's homes or in large, grass-lined pits that were dug

Below: A Native American teenager picks ears of corn in a field in Taos, New Mexico.

into the ground. Because corn ears are hard and dry well, they can be stored for many years. Scientists have found tiny, teosinte-like corn cobs that are 7,000 years old.

Native Americans throughout North America cooked corn with wood ashes from the fire or with a kind of mineral called lime. This way of cooking corn makes the outer layer of the kernel softer. It also makes the corn more nutritious, or good for you, by releasing nutrients that are in corn. At left, a woman in Mexico cooks corn sprouts in a pot to make a corn beer, called *tesguino*.

Left: This drawing shows ancient Peruvians storing their corn. The cobs were put into holes dug into the ground and lined with stone. Once full, they were covered with sand.

A Mother's Gift

The Penobscot Indians of Eastern North America say that corn is a gift of the First Mother. The ancient people, they say, lived by hunting alone. Soon there were not enough animals. People died of hunger. To make food for her children, the First Mother asked her husband to kill her and drag her body over the ground. She told him that he was to bury her bones in the middle of a field and go away for seven months. With great sadness, her husband did as she wished. When he and the children returned seven months later, the field was filled with tall, green, tasseled corn plants. The corn they ate was First Mother's flesh, sweet and healthful.

Above: An ancient clay object from Peru shows a god with three heads and a body made of corn ears.

Left: The shape of corn ears are cut into an Aztec stone altar. An altar is a table or platform found in a temple.

Right: This painting from a Mayan temple pictures a corn plant with ears that have human faces. The Mayans believed that the gods, after having created people from corn, gave them the plant to feed them and make them healthy.

Below: This mask made of corn straw was used by the Iroquois during gatherings of a group called the "Corn Husk Society."

23

Feeding the World

It is likely that you have eaten corn on the cob, cornbread, polenta, popcorn, or foods that are sweetened with corn syrup. If you have eaten meat, cheese, or eggs, you have eaten foods produced by corn-fed animals. Chances are you have used paste, paint, or drinking straws that were made from corn. Corn feeds the whole world.

Yet a large amount of land must be set aside to grow enough corn for all the chickens and cows we raise. Most of our gigantic cornfields grow where we have cut down forests, filled in marshes, or farmed meadows. Almost all of the corn we eat has been sprayed with poisons to kill corn pests like the corn borer. Some of that poison gets into our food. Corn has changed the world in many ways. Not all of these changes are for the better.

Above: Polenta is an Italian dish made from ground corn that has become popular throughout the world.

Below: A close-up of popocorn, which is made by heating corn kernels. Popcorn probably was first made in Mexico thousands of years ago.

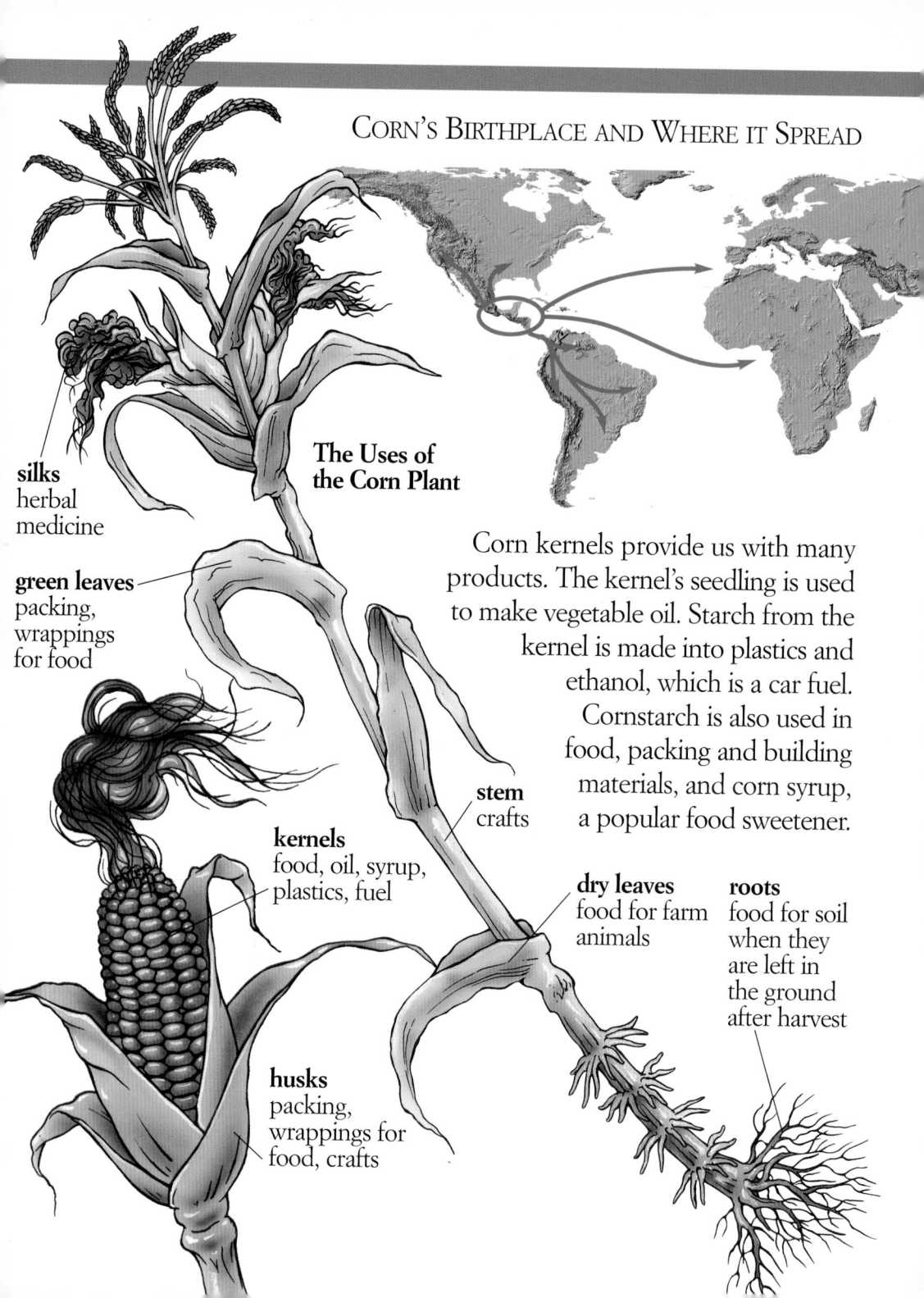

The Uses of the Corn Plant

silks
herbal medicine

green leaves
packing, wrappings for food

kernels
food, oil, syrup, plastics, fuel

stem
crafts

husks
packing, wrappings for food, crafts

dry leaves
food for farm animals

roots
food for soil when they are left in the ground after harvest

Corn kernels provide us with many products. The kernel's seedling is used to make vegetable oil. Starch from the kernel is made into plastics and ethanol, which is a car fuel. Cornstarch is also used in food, packing and building materials, and corn syrup, a popular food sweetener.

Glossary

anthers (AN-thurz) Sacs that contain a plant's pollen. The male part of the plant.

cereal (SEAR-ee-uhl) A grass that is grown for food.

chlorophyll (KLOR-uh-fill) A green substance in plants that uses energy from the sun to make sugar and oxygen from water and carbon dioxide.

domestication (DUH-mess-ti-KAY-shun) The process of making a kind of plant or animal more useful to humans.

embryo (EM-bree-o) Something in an early stage of growth and just beginning to be formed.

fertilization (FUR-tul-ih-ZAY-shun) The providing of the pollen's portion of the materials needed to produce a young plant.

internodes (IN-tur-nohdz) The parts of a stem that lie between its nodes.

larva (LAHR-vuh) An insect in its early life stage, which differs greatly from the adult stage.

minerals (MIH-ner-ulz) Natural substances from the soil that are needed by plants to stay healthy.

mutant (MEW-tant) A living thing that differs in some way from others of its kind.

nodes (NOHDZ) The thickenings of a plant stem from which leaves and branches grow.

ovule (OV-yule) The part of a female flower that carries the egg cell and grows up to become a seed if fertilized.

pith (PITH) Spongy matter in the stems of plants.

pollen grains (POL-in GRAYNZ) Tiny particles that carry a part of the material needed to produce a plant seed. A group of pollen grains is called pollen.

shank (SHANK) The thick stem that holds up the ear of corn and joins it to the plant's stem.

sheath (SHEETH) The thick branch from a corn stem that holds the ear of corn and produces husks.

silks (SILKS) Soft threads that lead each pollen tube to a single ovule.

tassel (TASS-el) The tall, curving branches that hold the male flowers of a corn plant.

vessels (VESS-uhls) Water-carrying tubes inside flowering plants. Vessels are made of many strong, hollow cells connected end to end.

Index

Web Sites

Due to the changing nature of Internet links, PowerKids Press has developed an online list of Web sites related to the subject of this book. This site is updated regularly. Please use this link to access the list:

www.powerkidslinks.com/gin/corn

About the Author

Andrew Hipp has been working as a naturalist in Madison, Wisconsin, since 1993. He is currently finishing his doctoral work in botany at the University of Wisconsin. Andrew and his wife, Rachel Davis, are collaborating on an illustrated field guide to common sedges of Wisconsin as they look forward to the birth of their first child.

Acknowledgments
This book draws on research and ideas of E. Anderson, J. Doebley, H. H. Iltis, E. J. Kahn Jr., S. H. Katz, G. Kuepper, Y. Matsuoka, M. Pollan, S. T. Ratcliffe, and their collaborators. The author gratefully acknowledges Dr. Iltis for reviewing a draft of this manuscript and providing extensive help with figures and book content.

Photo Credits